owns

Contents

Birds that live in towns and suburbs **7**
What brings the birds to town? 7
City centres 7
Unusual residents 8
Birds of the summer 9
Aerobatics 9
Warblers 9
Birdwatching in town 10
Sounds of the street 10
Nesting places 10
The winter months 11

Identifying the birds **13**
Shapes and sizes 13
Identifying brown birds 13
Some important do's and don'ts 16

Some of the birds that you might spot in towns **17**

The variety of bird life **48**
Breeding birds 48
One man's view 48
Town vagrants 48

Feeding the birds **51**
Natural foods 51
Feeding stations 51

Further information **52**
Societies to join 52
Birdsong recordings 52
Book list 52
Other reference books 53
Book series 53
Index 54

Birds that live in towns and suburbs

People tend to think of the countryside as the place where most birds live. But nowadays there is a large and growing population of birds who live the whole or part of their lives in towns and suburbs.

What brings the birds to town?

It is a fact that towns are several degrees warmer than the surrounding country on winter days and nights. This fact can mean survival to small birds. There is also a plentiful supply of food in and around towns – not only on garden bird-tables but in the general waste and overspill that happens in the everyday life of a town. And there is a considerable amount of 'country' in the town. There are parks and gardens, cemeteries, allotments and waste-ground. All these provide places where birds can feed, rest at night, and find nesting places.

City centres

Even city centres have a certain amount of bird life. Usually there will be a few sparrows, pigeons and starlings; birds which take advantage of human ways of life. They feed out of litter bins, on rubbish, and they sleep on the ledges of buildings. They have learned to tolerate close contact with human beings and even to cope safely with heavy traffic. It is not unusual to see pigeons feeding, absolutely unconcerned, while huge container lorries thunder by within feet of them.

◀ *The blue tit, a familiar bird of town and garden, and a less common resident, the nuthatch* ▶

The bird population of towns varies considerably throughout the year. The town is a permanent home for hardy urban sparrows, pigeons and starlings, and also for blackbirds, thrushes, wrens and tits; birds which make their homes in the town's green places. Other species may come into town periodically, usually on cold wintry days. Flocks of finches from the country, for instance, will forage on the outskirts of towns and come to garden bird-tables which they ignore during summer when food is plentiful. From further afield, there are the migrant birds who fly in from overseas to spend part of the winter or summer in Britain. A proportion of these migrants find their way into towns where conditions are suitable for them.

Black redstart and young.

Unusual residents

One of the most interesting town dwellers is the black redstart. This little bird in the thrush family was once only rarely seen in Britain. Over the last thirty years, it has been found more frequently, and always in town sites.

Black redstarts seem to have a taste for the industrial landscape. They look astonishingly at home in a disused gas-works or factory. On a rusty black piece of ironwork, the black and red plumage matches perfectly. The jutting ledges make good songposts and nest sites and there is food all around for the birds in the form of ground and flying insects.

A survey made a few years ago showed forty-seven black redstart pairs nesting in and around London; in power stations, timber yards, railway sidings, riverside warehouses and sites due for demolition.

Birds of the summer

There are some surprises in our everyday surroundings. We may miss seeing birds simply because we don't know they are there and don't look out for them. There are the migrants who visit Britain for the summer months who are, for the most part, insect-feeders.

Swifts, swallows and a number of warblers are seen in towns a great deal more these days. The clean air laws and other anti-pollution operations are at least partly responsible for this welcome increase in bird life. Both the birds and the insects they feed on live and breed more healthily and vigorously in the cleaner atmosphere.

Swifts, swallows and martins may now be seen dipping and diving in the sky even over the centres of cities. These birds are perhaps the most spectacular fliers of all as they hunt through the skies, the swift with stiff powerful wingbeats, the swallow more delicate and spidery with its long tail streamers. The house-martin is smaller and fluttery, with a bright flash of white on its back and breast.

Aerobatics

Spotted flycatchers also catch insect food in the air but they have a different style of aerobatics. They flip themselves into the air from a fencepost or branch, make a short whirling flight and return to the same perch. The spotted flycatcher may be seen quite often in town gardens, though you will have to look closely for the small upright grey shape.

Warblers

Warblers are another group of birds which do not force themselves upon one's attention. You are more likely to hear them than to see them. The beautiful cascade of the willow warbler's song will come from a small wooded area in a park or common. The fluting sounds of the blackcap waft down from many treetops in early summer. There is also the singing of the chiff-chaff whose song sounds almost exactly like its name. All these warblers are small brownish birds and they tend to be shy, often singing from within a tree or shrub.

A spotted flycatcher.

Birdwatching in town

Birdwatching in town requires rather a different approach from watching birds in the country. You won't, for instance, be taking out your boots and anorak, binoculars and a packed lunch for a day's expedition. In urban areas, bird-watching is much more a part of everyday life. It is what you can see from your window while you are having breakfast or doing the washing-up. It is the birds of a station or bus stop, the view into hidden places from the top of a double decker bus, or from a train. Sometimes you get a good long look, at other times, it's just a quick flash of wings. The important thing is to be aware. While everyone else is looking at their feet, you might be the only one to see a kestrel hovering over the high street.

Sounds of the street

In town as well as country, in spring and early summer, there is the morning bird concert, known as the dawn chorus. Anyone who can get up fairly early and take a walk about the streets is likely to hear a good number of birds singing from their favourite vantage points. Many of these birds will be establishing breeding territory so if you make the same journey regularly, it is possible that you will come to recognise individual singers. A breeding territory is an area in which a pair of birds can comfortably make their nest without interference or crowding from other birds of the same species. The male bird 'maps' his territory by singing loudly from points all along the boundary.

There will certainly be sparrows squabbling on the roofs, perhaps a starling or blackbird perched on a television aerial or chimney-pot. There may be a thrush on a telegraph pole, a robin on a fence or a wren in a low bush.

As you watch the birds singing, you gradually learn their individual songs. As this happens you begin to recognise the bird from the song alone, even when the singer is hidden from view. However, it can be confusing at first. Sometimes so many birds are singing together that you can't pick out one from another. There are several very good bird song records which are listed on p. 52. These are a great help when you are first learning. (Most libraries stock these or will get them in on request).

Nesting places

As summer advances, turn your eye to the likely nesting spots of the town. You may see the mud cups of housemartin nests just under overhanging roofs. Swifts actually fly into the eaves, swooping with unerring accuracy into a space just below the roof. Sparrows will use any gaps in walls and roofs or old sheds. Corrugated iron roofing is particularly appealing to them, giving them a ready-made tunnel into which they can poke their untidy nests of grass and feathers.

A thick hedge is another good place to watch. Blackbirds and hedge sparrows favour a hedge for nesting and you may find wrens and thrushes in hedges or thick shrubs. Magpies and the rest of the crow family prefer tree sites. Town birds are adaptable creatures and will nest in any spot which looks suitable and answers their requirements: shopping bags, old kettles and pans, inside cars and buses. There is a long list of new-style nesting places and you may be observant enough to add some more. There is just as unlikely a catalogue of nesting materials. Many species make use of paper and plastic. A London flycatcher made its nest almost entirely from cigarette papers and wax matches instead of the traditional straw and cobweb and a heron in Nottinghamshire made the outer structure of its big nest out of pieces of wire.

The winter months

As autumn draws into winter, the summer visitors depart. The days grow colder and the birds become bolder in their habits. This is the time when a bird table is really important. Not only is food scarce in winter, but the birds are using up a lot of energy just in keeping warm and they need to feed well to replenish that energy and to stay alive.

A number of birds migrate to Britain during the winter. In the thrush family, there are the redwings and fieldfares which we don't see at all during the summer. There will also be extra blackbirds and thrushes from abroad. Kestrels, gulls and ducks also come over from colder parts of the continent to spend the winter in Britain. Some of these migrants will come to the towns and the population will be further increased by the birds of the surrounding countryside drifting in for food and warmth. Places to watch are docks, dumps and weedy waste ground, parks and spots where there is water.

A blackbird that has made her nest in a coil of wire.

swift
swallows
kestrel
blackbird
black-headed gull
starling
tufted duck
house sparrow
pied wagtail

Identifying the birds

Shapes and sizes

Working out an identification for the birds you see is something which becomes easier once you've done it a few times and begin to know what to look for. At first, you may fail to notice the details which are mentioned in your field guide or identification book. To avoid this, try watching for the distinguishing features each time you see a bird. Check off as many of the features listed below as you can:

size – as big as a sparrow, duck, crow etc.
shape – duck shape, finch shape etc.
voice – song, alarm call notes, other noises
legs – colour, length etc.
feet – big, small, webbed etc.
beak – long, curved etc.
head – distinctive colour, eye stripe etc.
wings – white (or colour) wing bar in flight
tail – long, upright, white mark in flight etc.
colour – any special markings on breast, wing etc.
gait – run, hop, walk, shuffle
flight – awkward, swooping, fast, high
behaviour – feeding, courting etc.

Learning to identify birds is not an end in itself. It is a way of getting to know the birds you are watching. Knowing the name of a bird puts you in touch with what other people have seen and written, but you will also see things that are not in the books and begin to build up a picture of your own.

Of course, real birds will not stay as obligingly still for you as the illustrations in this book.

Identifying brown birds

Many of our birds are small brown creatures, difficult to tell, at first, from each other; brown is a good camouflage colour. Below is a list of brownish birds with a few hints on identification.

hedge sparrow (or dunnock) (*14.5cm. All measurements are from the beak to the tip of the tail*) shuffling walk/hop – delicate thin beak – no white in tail

house sparrow (*14.5cm*) bold hops – thick beak
♂ grey on head – black smudgy bib
♀ all pale grey/brown – pale eye-stripe

(♂: male; ♀: female; sexes alike where not otherwise indicated)

chaffinch
(*15cm*)
♀ brownish – white shoulder patch – white wingbar

linnet
(*13.5cm*)
♀ pinky brown – white wing bar, shows in flight and at rest – dancing flight

wren
(*9.5cm*)
very small – chestnut brown – tail flick upright – quick restless movements – flight low to the ground, whirring

skylark
(*18cm*)
pale brown – white outer feathers in tail – white underparts – crest on head – vertical flight

blackbird
(*25cm*)
♀ dark brown – strong pointed beak – hops – faint freckling of breast

song thrush (*23cm*) brown on back – creamy freckled breast

redwing (*21cm*) dark brown back – creamy white eyestroke – red underwing and flanks

missel thrush (*27cm*) grey-brown back – breast with blotches rather than freckles

Some important do's and don'ts

Do make a bird table and try to put out some nuts, coconuts and other food during winter.

Do put water out for birds in summer.

Don't bother to put out food in the late spring and summer, especially not coconut because baby birds can't digest it.

Don't ever provide desiccated coconut (the shredded kind) because birds can't digest it.

Don't rush to rescue baby birds. When young birds leave the nest, they flop about learning to walk and fly. Their parents will almost certainly find them and they can care for the fledglings much better than you can.

Do watch any baby bird you have found from a distance and see that it stays out of danger (from cats etc.). It may look lost but it is probably quite all right and human interference is much more likely to kill a fledgling than to help it. If you can't wait around and you think the bird is in danger, carefully lift it up and place it in a safer position on a ledge or in the crotch of a tree, where its parents will find and feed it.

Don't frighten the baby bird by chasing it about in your efforts to put it somewhere safe.

Do, if you think a baby bird is in danger, try to find a scarf or towel and throw it over the bird. You can then lift it to safety with as little fuss as possible.

The Royal Society for the Protection of Birds think this message is so important that they have put it on a poster.

Some of the birds that you might spot in towns

1

2

1 & 2 House sparrow *Passer domesticus* 14.5cm (beak to tip of tail)

This is one bird you should have no difficulty in spotting. They have lived with human beings for a long time.

Sparrows have thick strong beaks which can cope with seeds with thick husks. In summer, they also eat greenfly and hunt midges in the air.

The house sparrow is more at home in towns than in the countryside. Sparrows nest in all kinds of places: roofs, ventilators, pipes, holes in walls or trees. Listen in springtime for the chirrupy sparrow song and look out for sparrow pairs searching out nesting sites.

Towards autumn, watch and listen for the sparrow roosts, usually a tree where large numbers of birds will gather and chirp loudly together before night falls.

The top picture is of a male sparrow, the bottom is a female.

3

4

3 & 4 Starling *Sturnus vulgaris*
21.5cm

Starlings are not immediately appealing birds. They have a wicked-looking sharp beak and move with a quick jerky swagger. Don't dismiss them though. Look at the lovely metallic sheen on the dark plumage spangled with pearls of white, and at the strength of that pointed beak as it probes the ground for insects.

Out of the breeding season, starlings like company at night, and their evening roost can number many thousands. A roosting flock stopped Big Ben from striking one night by perching on the minute hand and preventing it from moving.

Before they go to roost, starlings make complicated group flights. They then alight on trees or buildings with a deafening twittering, which often exceeds the noise of the passing traffic.

5

5 Woodpigeon *Columba palumbus* 41cm

Spot this pigeon by the white patch on the neck and the white bar on each wing in flight. Listen for the soothing 'coo-*coo*, coo,coo-coo' (usually in rhythmic groups of five notes). Often seen in parks and large gardens, this pigeon is a voracious eater. The stomach of one was found to contain 163 peas and 3oz spinach.

6

6 Rock dove (feral pigeon) *Columba livia* 33cm

This sturdy bird is to be found in town centres as well as suburbs. It roosts and sometimes builds its nest on the ledges of large buildings. The plumage varies considerably, but all birds make a triple 'coo,roo,coo'.

7

7 Collared dove *Streptopelia decaocto* 32cm

As short a time ago as 1952, this pigeon was a rare sight in Britain but nowadays its harsh 'coo,*cooo*, cuk' may be heard in many cities particularly in the Midlands.

8

9

8 & 9 Blackbird *Turdus merula* 25cm

One of the most delightful songs you can hear in the town is the lovely rich melody of the blackbird. The alarm call is a sharp loud 'chink-chink-chink!'

The blackbird is a familiar visitor to lawns, occasionally pausing between hops to cock its head and listen before thrusting its beak into the ground to find an insect or worm. You can often hear blackbirds in ditches and shrubberies, as they rustle about, searching for insects under dead leaves.

In autumn they will eat fruit and berries from gardens and hedgerows. If you have a compost heap you will also see both blackbirds and starlings sorting through the waste, flinging aside bits of peel and eggshell to uncover more tasty morsels, a worm or spider or a piece of fruit.

In towns blackbirds will look for nesting places in a hedge, low tree or perhaps on the sheltered ledge of a building.

10 & 11 Berries and seeds

Elder, roses and many other garden and parkland shrubs provide a good source of food for birds during the autumn months. Elder is a great favourite with a number of birds and a bush may be completely stripped of its blue-black berries in a matter of hours.

Birds such as thrushes, blackbirds, redwings and starlings are very fond of berries and will eat not only the varieties that they find in the wild, but also garden varieties like the rosehips in the picture. Among the other fruits and berries they appreciate are yew berries, hawthorn, holly, and ivy berries.

10

11

12 Redwing *Turdus iliacus* 21cm

This winter visitor often keeps company with the other thrush-family migrants, the fieldfares. Combined flocks may be seen feeding on fields and large stretches of grass. The redwing tends to venture further into towns than the fieldfare and may sometimes be seen on grassy places in busy parts of towns.

Redwings look like small slim thrushes but they have a distinctive pale eyestripe and conspicuous patches of red beneath the wing and on the flank. These warmly coloured birds make a pleasant sight in the bleak winter months. In early spring, usually about March, the redwings fly off to their summer haunts in Russia and Scandinavia.

12

13

14

13 & 14 Song thrush *Turdus philomelos* 23cm

This bird, our commonest thrush, is resident throughout the year. Watch for the flash of its creamy freckled breast as it hops through the grass in search of worms, snails and insects. In autumn and winter it will take berries and fruit as well.

As the song thrush flies off you get a predominantly brown impression. There is no white in its tail.

The song thrush is one of the foremost singers in the urban chorus. Its song is sweet and piercing and it repeats each phrase two or three times over.

The four gaping song-thrush youngsters are probably nearly ready to leave the nest. They are well-feathered and their freckles are beginning to show. Those gaping orange mouths are said to act as a feeding signal to the parent birds. Both parents help with the feeding and they will go on giving the fledglings food for some time after they have left the nest.

15 Missel thrush *Turdus viscivorus* 27cm

The missel thrush is a big bird with dark patches rather than freckles on its breast. It looks greyish as it flies and has a flash of white on its tail and underwing.

The missel thrush is more of a fruit feeder than the song thrush. Yew and rowan are particular favourites but it likes rosehips, holly, ivy and hawthorn too.

It has a loud song, rather more strident than the song thrush, and not repetitive.

15

16 Skylark *Alauda arvensis* 18cm

The high, bubbling song of the skylark is one of the best sounds of summer. The British skylarks, like many birds, only sing during the breeding season. In winter their numbers are increased by migrants.

The skylark is suffering from the way towns are becoming more built up, with few open areas. Skylarks nest on the ground and this makes them easier to disturb than hedge or tree-nesting species.

16

17

18

17 & 18 Robin *Erithacus rubecula* 14cm

This bright-breasted little bird sings in winter as well as spring and summer, which is probably one of the reasons why the robin is a symbol of Christmas. Listen for the clear fluting song and for the rapid 'tic-tic-tic' of the alarm call, which sounds a bit like a typewriter in the distance.

Robins enjoy a varied diet of insects, fruits and berries. They are bold by nature and hop jauntily about parks and gardens, often quite close to people.

The greatest enemy to young robins is the cat. Many birds die in their first year, but research carried out with robins shows that the older a robin is, the wilier and better at surviving it becomes. The oldest known wild robin lived to the grand age of eleven years.

19 Hedge sparrow (or dunnock) *Prunella modularis* 14.5cm

Hedge sparrows have an odd half-hopping, shuffling gait and they keep mainly to the ground except when singing. They are likely to be seen feeding beneath the bird table, pecking up small crumbs left by other birds.

Hedge sparrows have slim small beaks, not nearly as powerful as those of house sparrows. In winter they feed mostly on weed seeds but in summer will take insects too.

20 Greenfinch *Carduelis chloris* 14.5cm

This is another bird which is increasingly seen in towns. Bold and pert in its movements, the greenfinch is a frequent visitor to gardens, especially those where its favourite food, *unsalted* peanuts, has been put out. Greenfinches also eat seeds, berries, fruit-tree buds and some insects.

They nest in trees, even sometimes the trees of streets. They are resident birds but tend to move about quite a lot, out of the breeding season.

19

20

21 Goldfinch *Carduelis carduelis* 12cm

This bright bird may be found flitting about waste-ground, dumps and allotments, in fact anywhere that it can find its main diet, seeds. Not an inner city bird, the goldfinch frequents large gardens, parks, and outer suburbs.

Goldfinches love thistle seeds and those of other flowers in the daisy family, and they will eat tree seeds and a few insects too. They make their nests in trees as a rule although one pair was recorded nesting in a large brussels sprout plant. When the young are fledged they fly with the parents in a family group. In late summer such family parties are a common sight, picking their way delicately over thistles, making their tinkling, twittering sounds as they go.

A band of goldfinches is known aptly as a 'charm'. In winter they often fly together in a large flock with other finches.

21

22

23

24

22–24 Linnet *Acanthis canabina* 13.5cm

Like the goldfinch, the linnet has a taste for wasteland where it feeds off weed seeds. It eats a very large range of seeds with a few insects as well in summer. The young are fed a high-protein diet of butterflies, flies and spiders as well as regurgitated seeds.

Nesting is usually well under way by the middle of May. Linnet nests are seldom far from the ground, usually in gorse, bramble or thorn bushes. The parent birds may raise two or even three broods with four to six eggs in each.

Linnets are not typical birds of the town although they seem to be coming into urban areas to feed more than they used to. In winter the numbers are greatly increased by migrant birds.

Linnets are sociable birds. They will fly together in family parties and in the colder weather associate in mixed flocks with greenfinches, goldfinches and yellowhammers.

The male in breeding plumage has striking red patches on his forehead and breast; at other times he is pinky-red. The hen and young birds are a streaky grey-brown. When they fly, both sexes show white on the wing and tail. They have the quick undulating flight typical of finches. They are alert, busy birds, hardly ever still as they flutter around the weeds. As they fly they give twittering calls which sound rather like 'linnet-linnet-linnet'.

25

26

25 & 26 Chaffinch *Fringilla coelebs* 15cm

Both sexes have a white shoulder patch and creamy-buff wing bars which show at rest and in flight. They also have white outer tail feathers. The male (25) is more colourful than the female with his blue-grey head and pink cheeks and chest. The female (26) is a yellow-brown with pale underparts.

When chasing off intruder chaffinches, the male puffs himself up and expands his white shoulder patch in an aggressive display. The female begins building the nest in late April or May. The nest is usually built near to the ground and a cover of lichens and birch bark helps to hide it.

Chaffinch food consists of three-quarters vegetable matter, the rest is mostly insects. They eat weed seeds and tree buds, berries and beech nuts and they enjoy kitchen scraps too. Chaffinches catch insects on the wing as well as on the ground and in trees.

27 Jackdaw *Corvus monedula* 33cm

You can often hear the sharp 'jic jac' cry of the jackdaw amongst the hoarse caws of rooks. Jackdaws feed on the ground, moving with a quick jaunty walk over park and garden. They like a wide variety of foods, from seeds to frogs and insects, and in towns they find litter bins hold some nice titbits.

Jackdaws are very sociable birds – if one member of the group is in trouble the rest will go to its aid.

Migrant birds who just stay for the winter fly away about April and the resident population begins looking for nesting sites. These are usually old buildings, holes in trees, chimneys, roofs and church towers.

28 Jay *Garrulus glandarius* 34cm

This member of the crow family has an untypically colourful plumage – and an unmistakable strident cry.

Town jays can often be seen at close quarters. They will perch watchfully, or make a rather ungainly exit, hopping over the ground, sometimes fanning the tail or raising the crest on the head. Make a sudden movement though, and the bird vanishes with a quick flash of its white rump.

Like the jackdaw, jays like both fruit and insects; they also eat nuts and often raid gardens and allotments for peas, beans and fruit. The jay is also a brazen egg robber.

27

28

29

30

29 & 30 Great tit *Parus major* 14cm

These attractive birds are among the boldest of bird visitors to the garden. They will nearly always be among the firstcomers to visit bird tables and will come right up to windows if peanuts or coconuts are hung close by.

Great tits are alert to danger and quick to assess it. They will feed with apparent unconcern from the safety of a bird table, though a cat may be sharpening its claws immediately beneath. Yet in other circumstances they treat cats with caution.

The great tit is conspicuous with its black frontal stripe standing out against a yellow chest. Close-up you can see the green back and a white stripe on the blue-grey wings. It is more difficult to be certain of identification by sound alone. The great tit has a wide variety of calls. One of its most common calls is a shrill couplet of notes which sounds like 't-teacher-teacher-teacher'.

31 & 32 Blue tit *Parus caeruleus* 11.5cm

Confusion between the two tits is unlikely: the blue tit is smaller and has a blue cap.

On the breast, there is a vague patch instead of a bold black streak. The small sharp beak is a menace to insect pests of the garden such as plant lice, weevils and larvae. Blue tits also enjoy seeds and nuts and like the great tits will take every advantage of bird tables, doing amazing acrobatics to get at hanging baskets of nuts or fat.

Like the great tits, the plumage of the male and female blue tits is similar, though the female is a little paler in colour. Their call is a high pitched wheezy 'tsee-tsee tsu-su-su' and a much crosser, harsher version of this is known as 'the scold'.

Blue-tits will search widely for food and their habit of roosting together in sheltered places gives them an extra protection from the winter cold.

31

32

33

34

33–35 Black headed gull
Larus ridibundus 35–38cm

All the illustrations on these two pages are of the same species. The smudgy head and the dark mark behind the eye is typical winter plumage for adult black-headed gulls. Summer dress is a sleek chocolate brown hood. Immature youngsters (pictured opposite) lack the dark head and have a spot like the winter adults. The wings are a soft mottled brown.

This is the gull you are most likely to come across if you live inland. Only sixty or so years ago, the sight of gulls away from the sea in the summertime was a rare occurrence. Nowadays it is not unusual to see hundreds of black-headed gulls inland at any time of the year. Many of these feed and live in or near to towns.

They may be seen on docks, rubbish tips, and reservoirs, or simply winging overhead keeping a sharp lookout for any sign of a source of food. They like a varied diet: fish, insects, meat and household waste. They usually spend the day feeding and then fly back to the communal roosting place of a large flock in the evening. They like to sleep on or by the water, so the roost is likely to be a reservoir, estuary, large lake or gravel pit.

35

When the breeding season comes round in spring, the birds choose a freshwater island or a piece of marshland where they form a breeding colony. Black-headed gulls have only one brood each year. Both parents incubate the eggs and feed the young. The young fly at five or six weeks. By mid-summer, the birds are making their way back from the breeding ground to their town and country haunts. In the last few years, there have been instances of gull pairs making their nests upon flat roofs in towns and suburbs.

Black-headed gulls are smaller and more delicate than most other gull species. Herring gulls and black-backed gulls are also seen inland (usually in winter); these all have heavier wedge-shaped beaks which are yellow in colour. Black-headed gulls have bright red legs and beaks.

36

37

36–37 Mallard *Anas platyrhynchos* 58cm

When the tame mallards in parks come up to take bread from your hand it is difficult to believe that it may be hard to get within 400 metres of the shy wild mallard. It is unlikely that wild ducks will rest on park ponds, but they will winter on a sizeable lake in a town or a reservoir or sewage farm.

Park mallards have a number of colour variations: the pure white farmyard duck is a kind of mallard and so are the brown Khaki Campbells. True mallard drakes have a white collar between the green head and the chestnut-purple chest. Note too the curly tail feathers. The duck is brown, but like the male she has a large blue *speculum* or wing-bar.

The mallard is the only duck which actually quacks – and it is the female which makes this familiar sound. The male makes a softer 'quek quek' and he whistles when he is courting.

38 Mute swan *Cygnus olor* 152cm

Mute swans died out as a wild species in Britain and today's birds are descendants of birds which were kept in captivity long ago.

They are devoted parents, assiduously caring for their young, though occasionally a cygnet will fall prey to a fox. They feed on weeds, bank reeds and grasses, which they reach for with those long elegant necks.

39 Wren *Troglodytes troglodytes* 9.5cm

The wren is not a shy bird, but it is very quick in its movements and will not stay long in one place. It has a tiny rotund body, a pertly cocked tail and a long sharp insect-catching beak.

It has an extremely loud rattling song which can sound like clockwork, one note following the last in unbelievably quick succession; it has been timed at 56 notes in just over 5 seconds.

38

39

40

41

42

40 & 41 Coot *Fulica atra* 38cm

A quarrelsome bird of larger lakes and ponds the coot can also be seen by canals and on the river bank. It may easily be picked out by its long white forehead and bill. It is a diving bird, feeding on water weeds which grow beneath the surface.

Coots don't fly very well and often dive to escape danger. They take a little jump to give impetus to the dive, and they can stay underwater for about a minute though it is usually less than this.

The young of both coot and moorhen are dark, downy and active. The baby coot has an orangey head.

42 Moorhen *Gallinula chloropus* 33cm

Moorhens are smaller than coots and have bright red foreheads, and bills with a yellow tip. Male and female look alike.

As it swims and walks the moorhen bobs its head. In the take-off before flight, it runs along the surface of the water for several metres before 'lift-off'. Moorhens feed along watersides, on weeds, grasses and seeds and a few insects and worms as well.

43 Tawny owl *Strix aluco* 38cm

Very much a bird of night, the tawny owl is rarely seen before dusk. But listen at night, by a park or cemetery and you are quite likely to hear their 'ke-wick, ke-wick' cries, or a soft 'hoo-hoo-hoo' (or as the storybooks have it 'tu-whit, tu-whoo').

Tawny owls do reasonably well in urban areas (though loss of habitat with elms dying from Dutch elm disease may affect them). They spend the day, perched upon branches of trees, high up and close to the trunk where foliage or ivy give cover. They are then virtually invisible from the ground. Tawny owls nest in trees, usually in a hole or in the old nests of other birds. Most large urban parks will have pairs of them.

43

Tawny owls hunt by night on their large rounded wings which beat noiselessly through the air. They will feed upon a wide range of creatures: young birds, mice and other small rodents, worms, snails, beetles and frogs.

44 

45 

46 

47 

44 & 45 Spotted flycatcher
Muscicapa striata 14cm

Though it does not have brilliant plumage, the flycatcher is a very exciting bird to see. As its name suggests, it feeds mainly on flying insects which it catches in a marvellously acrobatic figure-of-eight flight.

The spotted flycatcher is a summer visitor which breeds here, and it seems to be on the increase in towns. The young usually hatch out during June and the winter migration to Africa occurs between July and October.

46 Willow warbler
Phylloscopus trochilus 11cm
Among the summer visitors to Britain are several members of the warbler family. Though these tiny birds look alike, their songs are all quite different. Listen for the willow warbler in wooded places from mid-April onwards. The willow warbler song is one of the best sounds of spring, a delicate trilling fountain of notes on a downward scale.

47 Chiffchaff *Phylloscopus collybita* 11cm
This bird looks very similar to the willow warbler, but its song is easy to recognise. Its name tells you the sounds to listen for, in trees and shrubby places from mid-March onwards. It sings 'chiff-chaff, chiff-chaff'. This bird stays on a little longer than the willow warbler, not usually departing for Africa until November.

48

48 Kestrel *Falco tinnunculus* 34cm
One of the most exciting sights of the modern town scene is this beautiful falcon, hovering, almost still in the air. Most towns boast several places where you can be almost certain of seeing kestrels. Usually these are not the most salubrious spots: rubbish tips, waste land or over banks beside major roads. They hover in the sky, looking downwards with a fierce gaze for small mammals, such as mice and voles, or for small birds. They will also eat beetles and worms.

The male kestrel has a blue-grey head and tail and a black-spotted chestnut back. The female's chestnut and black extends over most of the top of her body; underneath both sexes are buff with dark streaks.

49 Housemartin *Delichon urbica* 12.5cm

If you have an oldish house with eaves, you may well be lucky enough to have house martins nesting beneath your roof. They are very much town birds as the Latin word 'urbica' (from the Latin *urbs* meaning 'town') signifies.

Housemartin flight is high and fluttery. Watch out for the white underparts and rump and the wide forked tail. They often fly in company with swifts and swallows, especially over water, where the insects are thickest. The return to Africa takes place throughout the autumn.

50 Swift *Apus apus* 16.5cm

Swifts, perhaps more than any other birds are masters of the air. It is thought that they actually sleep on the wing and that they only come down to land to nest.

They may be seen in summer, their strong scythe-like wings seeming to slice the sky, their harsh screams lingering on the air.

Swifts are bigger and stronger than martins or swallows, and they are sooty-brown all over.

51 Magpie *Pica pica* 46cm

Compare the magpie with the jay on p. 29. Despite the difference in colour, do you see a resemblance in the general air of robustness and the strong beak? Magpies and jays both belong to the crow family. Magpies feed on all kinds of things: insects, young birds, small mammals, eggs, snails, worms and fruits, nuts and berries.

Magpies are becoming more numerous in towns and may often be seen in gardens, sometimes coming to bird tables, where they dominate the scene with their huge size. The magpie has a loud and strident cry, something like a wicked cackling laugh.

Magpies usually nest in trees, sometimes in thorny bushes. The nest is very individual, with a domed roof of twigs and thorns. Both male and female build the nest.

52 Carrion crow *Corvus corone* 47cm

This splendid crow is black all over. It feeds mainly on the ground, often on open parkland. It has a strong flight with slow powerful wingbeats. Crows often perch watchfully in trees.

They are solitary birds, and are usually seen in ones or twos rather than flocks, except at the roost.

They have a wide taste in food, with more or less the same diet as magpies. One curious refinement is that carrion crows will drop hard-shelled food such as snails or nuts, from a height to smash it open.

53 Rook *Corvus frugilegus* 46cm

The old saying goes, 'If there's lots of crows, they're rooks and if there's only one rook, it's a crow.' Which means that rooks are usually found in groups and crows singly.

At a first glance you could easily mistake rooks and crows, but on closer acquaintance you find that

53

they are very different. The rook has a white face, and its bill is more slender and less curved. The rook also has loose feathers on its flank which hang down, making it look as if the bird is wearing baggy trousers.

Rooks do not inhabit heavily built-up areas but sometimes spend winters in town parks. They may often be seen feeding by the sides of motorways and major roads. They eat mainly vegetable food, with a few insects as well.

54

54 Swallow *Hirundo rustica* 19cm

Another graceful flier and a bird of summer, the long tail-streamers make the swallow distinctive from a distance. Close-up you can see the soft peach-coloured underparts and the chestnut throat and forehead.

Like swifts and martins, swallows feed on insects as they fly. They sometimes settle on telegraph wires and buildings, especially in the autumn, when large twittering groups will perch together restlessly before taking off on their long migration to Africa.

55 Great crested grebe
Podiceps cristatus 48cm

This beautiful grebe is one of the most striking inhabitants of lakes and reservoirs. When they are breeding the birds have a black double-horned crest of feathers and a wide 'frill' or 'ruff' of chestnut and black feathers which spreads out over the 'chin'. They have long slender necks and a breast of dazzlingly white soft feathers.

In early spring, the grebes start their elaborate, head wagging and weed swapping courtship. Their floating nest, made of weeds, is moored among the reeds of the water's edge. When the babies are hatched, the adults will sometimes carry them upon their backs. Like most baby birds the young grebes are very hungry and the adults have a hard time diving for enough fish to feed them.

56 Dabchick or **little grebe**
Tachybaptus ruficollis 27cm

The dabchick belongs to the same family as the great crested grebe, and is also known as the little grebe. It is sometimes seen on canals and rivers, but it is very shy and will dive underwater and hide in the reeds or bank vegetation at the slightest hint of danger. The little grebe is rotund in shape with a short straight bill, but it has no crest.

57 Tufted duck *Aythya fuligula* 43cm

The large patch of white on the side of the male tufted duck means that you can spot it at a distance. It also has a 'pigtail' of feathers growing from the back of its head. The female's 'pigtail' is shorter, and she is brown all over. Both sexes have a grey-blue bill which is black-tipped, and they show a white wing-bar when they fly. Tufted duck dive for their food which is mostly aquatic weed, but also includes insects and molluscs. They are sociable birds and are usually found in flocks. The number of tufted duck increases in winter because of migrants; this is the time when they may be seen on the larger lakes of town parks and on reservoirs.

58

59

58 Pied wagtail *Motacilla alba* 18cm

These perky little birds with their long wagging tails are often known as 'water wagtails' because they are frequently found near fresh water. They feed mainly on insects and many of these are aquatic species of gnats and flies. Wagtails have a characteristic dipping flight and as they go by in their undulating flight, they call out 'chissick, chissick'. They are sociable birds and are usually seen in groups of six or so. At night they roost together in large numbers, particularly during the autumn months. They have been recorded roosting in sewage farms, and inside greenhouses. Pied wagtails breed all over Britain and Ireland; in the colder months they drift southwards.

59 Canada goose *Branta canadensis* 92–102cm

This large, black-necked goose has a white 'chinstrap' at the top of its long neck. It was introduced to Britain to grace the ornamental lakes of large estates, as long ago as the seventeenth century. It was only comparatively recently that they began to escape into the wild, and to live and breed independently of human beings. Canada geese are now probably the most common geese to be found in Britain. They seem to survive equally well in town or country and they breed on meres, marshes and rivers, as well as flooded gravel pits, reservoirs and town lakes.

60 Great spotted woodpecker
Dendrocopos major 23cm

The great spotted woodpecker is probably our most common woodpecker. It is a dramatic looking bird with black and white markings. The male has a bright red patch on the back of the neck. Both male and female have a red patch on the back, under the tail feathers. The female is black and white, without any red markings on the neck, but the young have a red 'cap' on the tops of their heads. The 'drumming' of the great spotted is sharp and brief, usually lasting for about a second at a time. It is made by a very rapid tapping with the beak, usually on a dead branch. They feed mainly upon the larvae of wood-boring insects, but also eat spiders, nuts, seeds and berries. Over the last thirty years this species has become much more common in suburban parks and town gardens. They usually bore their nests out of the bole of the tree high off the ground. They breed all over England, Wales and Scotland; like other woodpeckers, they have never been found in Ireland.

61 Nuthatch *Sitta europaea* 14cm

Nuthatches sometimes search for food with their heads pointing down the tree trunk; they search the tree trunks with jerky movements in all directions. They eat insects, nuts and seeds; they wedge the larger nuts and acorns into a crack and hammer at them with their stout beaks until they split.

They are very attractive – grey-blue on the back and wings and peach-coloured underneath, with a striking black eye-stripe. There is some white under the chin, and also in the outer feathers of their short tails. Nuthatches may sometimes be found in suburban parks and large gardens in central and southern England. They make their nests inside holes in trees, and often reduce the entrance size with mud.

62 Treecreeper *Certhia familiaris* 12.5cm

Tree-creepers also hunt for insects on the trunks of trees, but they always work their way upward, using their stiff tail feathers for support. The back and wings of the bird are brown and their wings are streaked with buff; the underparts are silvery white. The beak is long and curves downwards. They are very well camouflaged against the tree bark and are difficult to see. Treecreepers breed over most of Britain and Ireland and are to be found in many parks and sometimes in large gardens.

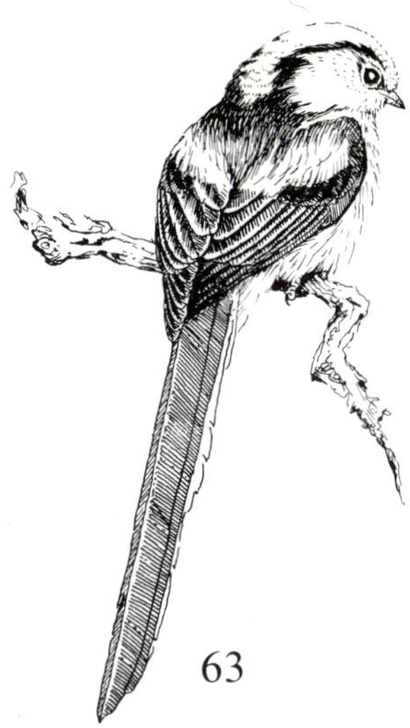

63

63 Long-tailed tit *Aegithalos caudatus* 14cm

Over half of the length of the long-tailed tit is composed of its tail. This species may often be seen in overgrown places and on scrubland. They are very pretty, fluffy little birds, black and white, with pink on their wings and underparts. They are sociable birds and are usually to be seen in groups, whistling and chattering to each other as they make their short flights from tree to tree, looking for insects to eat. Their nests are made of moss and lichens, with a soft lining of feathers. Several adult birds may care for one nest and the young.

64 Coal tit *Parus ater* 11.5cm

The coal tit may be distinguished from other black-headed tits by the clear white patch on the back of the neck. It has no markings on the breast which is pale buff-coloured, though it has a small black patch beneath its chin. The coal tit prefers coniferous trees, and is often to be found in parks and gardens where these grow. It is a small acrobatic bird, and will cling upside down to branches or pine cones, picking off insects and spiders, and sometimes eating seeds. Churchyards with yews, fir trees or cypresses provide a good habitat for town coal tits and it is worth listening carefully for their high, rasping calls.

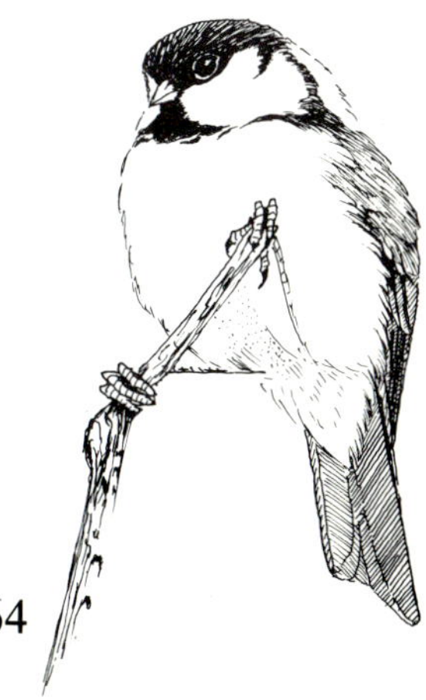

64

65

65 Goldcrest *Regulus regulus* 9cm

This is another bird which is associated with conifers – particularly yew trees – whose only habitats in towns may be churchyards and gardens with ornamental conifers. Goldcrests (and their relatives firecrests) are the smallest of all the British birds. The male goldcrest has a bright orange crown and the female has a yellow one, which is why these birds have the name *Regulus*, or 'little king'. It is not difficult to observe goldcrests, despite their small size, because they are very active and flick restlessly from branch to branch, picking out insects and spiders with their small, thin beaks; they advertise their presence with a high, thin, 'zzi, zi' buzzing cry.

66 Tree sparrow *Passer montanus* 14cm

Tree sparrows are much less common than house sparrows and far less closely associated with people. However, many suburban parks have a population of tree sparrows and it is worth giving any group of sparrow-like birds a second look in case there are some tree sparrows among them. Both male and female tree sparrows are similar in appearance with a chestnut brown head and a small black patch on the whitish cheek. The black throat bib is smaller than that of the male house sparrow. Tree sparrows are slightly smaller in size than house sparrows and more agile in their movements.

66

67 Black redstart
Phoenicurus ochruros 14cm

67

The black redstart is the only rare breeding bird in Britain which is mostly found in industrial and urban places. Both sexes have a red tail. The male is dusty black with a whitish patch on the wing, and the female is browny-grey all over, except for her tail. The small population of black redstarts is mainly concentrated in south-eastern England where it is to be found close to buildings, walls and waste ground near habitations. They feed mostly upon insects, spiders and millipedes, and berries in winter. The black redstart's song is a rapid warble which is interrupted at intervals by a harsh, metallic grinding sound.

68

68 Bullfinch *Pyrrhula pyrrhula* 15cm

The male bullfinch is a handsome and colourful bird. Its chin and breast are bright rose-red, and contrast with the pearl-grey of its back, and its black wings and tail. The female has a paler pink front. Both sexes have a white rump which flashes conspicuously when they fly. Bullfinches like scrubby ground with bushy tangles of undergrowth, which provide good nesting places for them. There are usually a few pairs in town gardens, parks and churchyards, but they are shy and, despite their bright colour, are often difficult to spot. They are regarded as a pest by gardeners because during the winter, when seeds are difficult to find, bullfinches will feed on the buds of fruit trees and shrubs.

The variety of bird life

Towns offer the observant bird-watcher a very wide variety of species that can be seen and studied. There are large numbers of breeding birds; there are winter visitors and the rare vagrants. The ornithological vagrants of the town are those birds whom one would not normally expect to find in an urban setting but who occasionally drift in, maybe spending a few days here or there, before flying off to more traditional surroundings.

Breeding birds

Many British breeding birds are residents, the thrushes, wrens and robins and so on, but the breeding population also includes the summer visitors, such as swallows, martins and warblers. A survey (carried out 1969–1970), called *Bird Life in the Royal Parks*, looked in particular at four parks in the vicinity of London. Between them these parks held no less than 64 breeding species. There are ducks, owls, woodpeckers, finches and tits, several kinds of warbler. There are redstarts, goldcrests and probably at least one pair of cuckoos.

One man's view

Eric Simms, an ardent and observant ornithologist, spent many years from childhood onwards in town and suburb and did much of his birdwatching in these surroundings. In the area near his home in Dollis Hill, a fairly well built-up district of north London, he has recorded 48 winter visitors and passage migrants. You would have to be a pretty keen birdwatcher to catch sight of many of these birds. But it's an inspiring list. Who wouldn't be prepared to get up at dawn to catch sight of a peregrine falcon? And wouldn't you be pleased to see a powerful great black-backed gull (with a wing span well over a metre) or to catch sight of the tiny goldcrest, no more than nine centimetres from tip to tail? The winter months are the time to look for wading birds that have come inland, curlews, with their down-curved bills, sandpipers, redshanks, and greenshanks with their haunting cries.

Town vagrants

Eric Simms has also seen an impressive number of vagrants, unusual wanderers who find their way into his suburb. The 25 species he has noted include little owl, bittern, heron, kingfisher, buzzard, sparrowhawk and woodcock. It is quite remarkable to think of these birds in urban surroundings. Yet it is not so unusual and it is well worth the while of any bird-watcher to look more closely at any bird who seems a little out-of-the-ordinary. Some birds actually appear to oblige ornithologists with their presence; there are stories of a hoopoe and of a golden oriole landing in the garden of a birdwatcher, who promptly photographed and recorded them. This is not so much of a coincidence as it seems. It's amazing what you can see if you are always alert for the unexpected happening.

The hoopoe: an exciting and unusual visitor, which may occasionally be seen in Britain.

Great tits have no problems with peanuts contained in a wire cage like this.

Feeding the birds

If you simply stock your bird table with kitchen scraps, you will probably find that all of the 'top ten' species will visit you. However, if you vary the food, you may well attract species with rather different tastes. String up peanuts, or put them shelled into a wire basket, hang up half a coconut, and some fat or suet. There are wild bird food mixtures which are sold commercially in pet shops and garden stores. *Never* use salted peanuts, only the natural kind – shelled or unshelled. These are very good, but expensive. The birds will also appreciate fruit, fresh or dried, that you put out. And don't forget that in winter when everything is frozen over, the birds need water just as much as they would do in a dry summer.

Natural foods

Birds will appreciate bits of bread and fat and coconut but it will be a slightly alien diet for them. It is a nice idea to try to provide something for them which is like their natural food. A wild patch of garden which has in it 'weed wildflowers' such as thistles, poppies, knapweed, ragwort, teasels and nettles will appeal to many birds, particularly goldfinches.

There is a long list of trees and bushes which are popular with birds for their nuts or berries. Among the favourites are yew, hazel, hawthorn, holly, lime, guelder rose and honeysuckle.

Probably one of the easiest and most comfortable ways of watching birds is from a window looking on to a garden. Even quite small town gardens can sport a number of different species.

Feeding stations

A 'feeding station' such as a bird table will draw birds to it and presents a focal point which is easy to observe. The 'top ten' birds which you could expect to come to an urban bird table are:

blackbird	greenfinch
starling	hedge sparrow (dunnock)
house sparrow	great tit
blue tit	song thrush
robin	chaffinch

Bird tables are useful items to have; you can position them somewhere suitable and put food such as bread and seed upon them and hang nuts, peanuts and fat around them. They are easy to buy or to make yourself. The most important thing to remember is that the support pole should be well off the ground and absolutely unclimbable by cats. You will want to position it to be in good view of the windows, but bear in mind that the birds will like it as much in the open as possible so that they can watch for danger. Make sure that it is too far from trees or ledges for cats to jump on, and remember that there could be danger below as well; food will drop to the ground and hedge sparrows and other birds will want to pick this up without being menaced by cats lurking in nearby undergrowth.

If you don't have a garden, there are many other places which could do as well. You could construct a ledge on a patio, or make use of an existing ledge or convert a window box into a bird feeding station.

Further information

Societies to join

The Royal Society for the Protection of Birds
The Lodge, Sandy, Bedfordshire
Concerned with conservation and protection of birds, the RSPB manages a number of bird reserves. Magazine *Birds* free to members.

Young Ornithologists Club
The Lodge, Sandy, Bedfordshire
National society for young people (aged seven to thirteen) who are interested in birds. Publishes a magazine called *Bird Life*.

Natural History Societies
Nearly every county in Britain has a local natural history society. Much very useful work goes on at this local level and the societies usually produce news sheets or magazines and organise field trips and lectures. A local library or town hall should be able to supply addresses.

Birdsong recordings

A very useful aid to familiarising yourself with birdsong. If you can't afford to buy them, see if you can borrow them from the library.

Back Garden Birds Town and garden species. Notes by Eric Simms. BBC recording.

British Garden Birds Songs and calls of twenty-five garden birds on two records with a short book by Peter Condor of the RSPB. Published by Record Books, available from RSPB, The Lodge, Sandy, Bedfordshire.

Listen . . . the birds Eighteen records, covering a wide number of species. From the RSPB.

Book list

The Birds of Britain and Europe, Heinzel, Fitter, Parslow (Fontana)
A good field identification book of European species.

The New Bird Table Book, Tony Soper (Pan)
A very useful, practical book about the birds you may see in your garden.

Watching Birds, James Fisher and Jim Flegg (Penguin)
An introduction to bird watching.

Birds of Town and Suburb, Eric Simms (Collins)
The bird life of towns, described and examined by this eminent ornithologist. Written for adults, but well worth dipping into, even if you don't read all of it.

Bird Count Humphrey M Dobinson (Penguin)
An introduction to ornithology and 'scientific' bird-watching with interesting information and bird surveys.

The Atlas of Breeding Birds in Britain and Ireland J T R Sharrock (T & A D Poyser)
The result of a country-wide survey of British and Irish birds, with fascinating maps and a readable text. This is worth borrowing if you can't afford to buy it.

Other reference books

Birds of Wood, Park and Garden, Lars Jonsson (Penguin Nature Guides)

Beginner's Guide to Bird Watching, Reg Harrison (Pelham)

Collins Guide to Bird Watching, R S R Fitter (Collins)

Collins Guide to British Birds, Fitter and Richardson (Collins)

A Field Guide to the Birds of Britain and Europe, Peterson, Mountford and Hollom (Collins)

Oxford Book of Birds, Campbell and Watson (Oxford)

RSPB Guide to British Birds, Saunders (Hamlyn)

RSPB Book of Garden Birds, Bennett (Hamlyn)

Book series

Black's Picture Information Book series

1 *Insects*
2 *Pond and Marsh*
3 *Seashore*
4 *Trees*
5 *Conservation*
6 *Flowers and their Visitors*
7 *Fungi*
8 *Pests*
9 *Animals and Plants in the Fields*
10 *Mountains, Plains and Rivers*
11 *Prehistoric Animals*
12 *What you can Find in a Park*
13 *Mammals in Britain*
14 *Wild Flowers of Verges and Waste Land*
15 *Heath and Moorland*
16 *Birds in Towns*

The Nature in Close-up series (A & C Black)

1 *The Life of a Butterfly*
2 *Newts*
3 *Food Chains*
4 *The Garden Spider*
5 *Honeybees*
6 *The Dragonfly*

Index

Berries and seeds 21
Bird tables 7,50-51
Black redstart 8,47
Blackbird 11,12,14,20
Black-headed gull 12,32-33
Blue tit 6,31
Bullfinch 47

Canada goose 43
Carrion crow 40-41
Chaffinch 14,28
Chiffchaff 39
Coal tit 45
Collared dove 19
Coot 36

Dabchick 42

Gardens 51
Goldcrest 46
Gold finch 26
Goose, Canada 43
Great tit 30,50
Great spotted woodpecker 44
Greenfinch 25-26

Hedge sparrow 13,24-25
Hoopoe 48-49
House sparrow 12,13,17
Housemartin 40

Jackdaw 28-29
Jay 29

Kestrel 12,39

Linnet 14,26-27
Long-tailed tit 45

Magpie 40
Mallard 34
Missel thrush 15,23
Moorhen 36-37
Mute swan 35

Nuthatch 7,44-45

Oriole, golden 48

Peanuts 51
Pied wagtail 43

Redwing 15,21
Robin 24
Rock dove 19
Rook 41
Royal Society for the Protection of Birds (RSPB) 16,52

Simms, Eric 48
Skylark 14,23
Song thrush 15,20
Spotted flycatcher 9,11,38
Starling 12,18
Swallow 12,41
Swan, mute 35
Swift 12,50

Tawny owl 37
Territory 10
Thrushes *missel thrush* 15,23; *song thrush* 15,20
Tits *blue tit* 6,31; *coal tit* 45; *great tit* 30,50; *long-tailed tit* 45
Tree sparrow 46
Treecreeper 14,45
Tufted duck 12,42-43

Weed wildflowers 51
Woodpecker, great spotted 45
Woodpigeon 19
Wren 14,35